Patterns in Emptiness

Understanding Dependent Origination in Buddhism

Lama Jampa Thaye

Patterns in Emptiness

Understanding Dependent Origination in Buddhism

Lama Jampa Thaye

RABSEL
PUBLICATIONS

RABSEL PUBLICATIONS
16, rue de Babylone
76430 La Remuée, France
www.rabsel.com
contact@rabsel.com

This project was supported by the DRAC and Normandy Region under the FADEL Normandie, France.

Contents

To my masters

Preface by
HH the 17th Karmapa Trinley Thaye Dorje

The 17th Karmapa Trinley Thaye Dorje

I am delighted to write this foreword for Lama Jampa Thaye's latest publication, "Patterns in Emptiness", which skilfully deals with the topic of dependent origination. This subject lies at the very heart of Buddha's teachings, and is central to an authentic understanding of the Buddha dharma.

In our present day and age, it is rare to find teachers like Lama Jampa Thaye, who succeed in presenting the complex teachings of the Buddha dharma in both a traditional and accessible manner.

This is no simple task: on the one hand, the Buddha's teachings need to be presented faithfully, without being diluted or transformed. On the other hand, the teachings are beneficial for everyone to understand, and so accessibility is key.

This is a challenge, because there is a tendency in contemporary English to simplify complex ideas, in order to inspire enthusiasm in the readers and make content more 'user-friendly'.

Therefore, it requires rare skill to utilise the means of the English language to convey the subject of dependent origination in an authentic manner, and at the same time engender enthusiasm in the readers by presenting it in a well-structured, approachable way. Lama Jampa Thaye excels in this regard.

Therefore, I am delighted to see that there is once again a work by Lama Jampa Thaye dealing with one of the central teachings of Buddhism.

May the readers gain both enjoyment and benefit from "Patterns in Emptiness".

With prayers

Karmapa Trinley Thaye Dorje
New Delhi
27th July 2018

Introduction

This present work is appearing as part of an intended series of short introductory texts on major topics in Buddhist philosophy. It is based on material from teachings that I gave in Dhagpo Kagyu Ling in France in the summer of 2017. Subsequently, Audrey Desserrières made a lightly edited transcript of these teachings, which I then worked on back in London, in between other duties.

Perhaps inevitably, given the subject matter, this book is in some ways a short introduction to Buddhism itself, as well as an examination of dependent origination. This seems appropriate because the Buddha's teaching themselves are, in their interconnected nature, a manifestation of the dependence which characterises our world.

The importance of understanding dependent origination for those who wish to practise Buddhism can hardly be overstated. It is no exaggeration to describe it as the antidote to the disorder in our thinking about the world – a disorder which leaves us alienated from that world and in the grip of disturbing emotions and projections. Without the clear understanding that comes from attention to this teaching, the attempt to utilise meditation techniques, up to and including the methods of Vajrayana, will be little more than exercises in fantasy and our 'compassion' will be merely a genuflection to the latest fashions in sentimentality and ideology.

Naturally, the presentation of dependent origination here reflects the teachings of my own masters. I was lucky enough to receive the transmission of the works of outstanding thinkers from the Sakya, Kagyu and Nyingma traditions, whose words I have cited in this work to illuminate the teaching. However, any errors are my own.

Finally, I would like to express my thanks to my wife Albena, my translator Audrey and my editor Benjamin Lister for their assistance in this work.

Lama Jampa Thaye

Chapter 1
The Significance of Dependent Origination

Every culture – every system of thought – offers answers to the profound questions of our existence: 'What is the source of suffering and what is the source of happiness?' 'Why are things the way they are in the world?' 'How best should we use our life?'

Some find the answer in a God or gods. Some say there is a plan. Some say everything has come about merely through physical evolution or random chance and some say there's no answer at all. In the Buddha's teaching, however, the answer lies in 'dependent origination'.

Dependent origination (Skt. *pratitya samutpada*) is one of the most important teachings given by the Buddha. One might even say that it is at the heart of his teaching, because it touches on so many other parts of his doctrine such as karma, rebirth, suffering, liberation and compassion. In fact, it is not really possible to make sense of those other teachings without understanding dependent origination. Equally importantly, Buddha's stress on dependent origination is what makes his tradition utterly distinct from all other systems of thought. Therefore, at a time when Buddhism is still relatively new in the West, it is vital that this teaching occupies a central place in the dissemination of the dharma.

The great philosopher Jamgon Ju Mipham explains the meaning of dependent origination as follows:

> Dependent origination means that nothing included within the category of inner or outer phenomena has arisen without a cause. Phenomena have also not originated from an independent cause, an uncaused and permanent creator such as self, time or God. The fact that phenomena are produced based on the interdependence of their respective causes and conditions is called dependent origination. To proclaim this is the unique approach of the Buddha's teaching.[1]

Despite this summary sounding somewhat technical, it would be mistaken to think that the teaching of dependent origination is merely a kind of philosophical idea about the world, an intriguing theory to toy with intellectually but without any consequence for our life and culture. We cannot deny that it is, of course, a type of philosophical thinking. However, just like all of the Buddha's teachings, the sole aim of his teaching of dependent origination is the elimination of suffering and bringing about happiness.

We can begin to understand the special role of the teaching of dependent origination when we consider the connection of dependent origination to the teachings contained in the first discourse given by the

Buddha after his enlightenment. In a garden close to Varanasi, Buddha's former companions from the time when he had sought enlightenment in ancient Indian traditions of yoga had asked him to expound to them the way to enlightenment. In response to their request, he taught his erstwhile companions, and now his first five disciples, the teaching which became known as 'The Four Noble Truths':

1. The truth of suffering
2. The truth of the causes of suffering
3. The truth of the cessation of suffering
4. The truth of the path that is the cause of that cessation.

The way in which these four truths relate to each other emphasises the importance, in the Buddha's teaching, of the *dependent* relationship between results and their causes. The Buddha explained that freedom from suffering (referred to in the first noble truth) cannot come about merely through faith or reliance upon some authority, but only by uncovering the causes that lead to that suffering (the second noble truth) and then by discovering the way to bring those causes to an end (the third and fourth noble truths). To understand these four noble truths, it is crucial that we understand dependent origination.

The roots of suffering lie in our misunderstanding of the nature of the world. It is this misunderstanding of the world that acts as the foundation of all the disturbing emotions that presently dominate our mind. It is those disturbing emotions which impel us to search for happiness. Yet, contrary to our hopes, however, the way in which we do so produces only suffering.

In our present state, we are deprived of happiness and confronted repeatedly with disappointment, disillusionment and misery. This state originates in dependence upon our ignorance about the nature of things. By 'ignorance' we mean, at its simplest, our mistaken attribution of permanence, happiness, selfhood and purity to phenomena that are, in actuality, impermanent, suffering, devoid of self and impure. At its most subtle, it is our grasping at reality as possessing any characteristic through which it may be captured by the dualistic mind. Such ignorance, in its gross and subtle forms, causes us to wrestle with the world in a futile struggle to acquire from it that which it cannot give us.

Therefore, the suffering that we experience in the cycle of birth and death (Skt. *samsara*) does not come about by random accident or chemical processes of the physical world or because some external entity is inflicting it upon us in order to punish us. The immediate source of our suffering is our erroneous actions, which lead us into continual conflict with a world that we cannot control by our wishes. We are not forced to accomplish those actions, nor do they just occur accidentally. Instead, they are prompted by the disturbing emotions of desire, hatred, ignorance and so on that themselves arise as a consequence of our fundamental misapprehension of the nature of the world. Such is the genealogy of suffering.

Thus the disturbing emotions are also not something that attacks us from outside like a disease. Instead, they have arisen in dependence upon our ignorance about the nature of the world. Suffering, actions and disturbing emotions are all dependent phenomena. All these things are part of a chain of causation which we must understand if we wish to become free from these disturbing emotions.

If this is how samsara, the world of suffering, arises, we might well ask: 'How does nirvana, the cessation of suffering, come about?'

Just like samsara, nirvana does not happen randomly, nor is it something that is imposed upon us from outside. Randomness would mean we are powerless to effect any change whatsoever, including bringing an end to suffering. Similarly, if things were determined by God we would be powerless, since everything would be determined by him. Nirvana, in its own nature, is unconditioned, but the ascertainment of nirvana is also a dependent phenomenon, in that nirvana depends on our practice of the threefold path of ethics, meditation and wisdom. Only through this path can we eliminate the disturbing emotions and ignorance, the causes of samsara. Thus the key to nirvana is in our own hands, if we understand dependent origination, since understanding dependent origination is the means to eliminate the disturbing emotions and ignorance.

In short, we do not need to search for an external agent or god to free us from samsara (the cycle of suffering) or bring us to nirvana (freedom from suffering). It is not any external agent, god or devil who has created samsara or nirvana. Their origin lies solely in dependence upon the causes that have just been outlined.

The great Indian master Nagarjuna, recognising this great significance of dependent origination, says:

This arising of dependent origination, the precious and
    Profound treasure of the teachings of the Conqueror
Whoever perfectly sees it
Knows reality as does the Buddha.[2]

Philosophically speaking, understanding dependent origination ensures that we will not fall into 'extreme views' – views which project a disordered understanding on to the world. As Buddha pointed out, one extreme is represented by the group of 'eternalist' views, which are notions of the world that assert the unchanging and unceasing existence of entities. Such views are characteristic of theistic religions. Buddha taught that the other extreme is represented by the cluster of views that one might label 'annihilationist', which propose that there is no connection between actions and results and that there are neither past nor future lives. Modern and ancient versions of materialism both belong to this grouping.

Followers of these extreme views lack any knowledge of dependent origination and thus exaggerate incomplete observations about the world into absolutes. The 'eternalists' exaggerate the element of continuity that exists between past, present and future into an absolute unchangingness and therefore elaborate theories such as the existence of an unchanging god, immortal souls, permanent selves and so on. At the other extreme, the 'annihilationists' exaggerate impermanence, and change impermanence into an absolute denial of any continuity at all and, consequently, deny karma and rebirth.

In contrast, the Buddha's view, the Middle Way view, transcends both reductive extremes, in asserting that all things come into being only through dependent origination. It provides an answer to the philosophical deadends of eternalism and materialism – dead-ends because final liberation from suffering is impossible through them. Yet, at the same time, although it is so profound in its meaning and liberating when truly understood, this view is simply in accord with the way the world really is: that causes and conditions continually interact and thus give rise to effects. Presently we are intoxicated with ideology, but dependent origination just describes the actual world in which we live, rather than the one that we imagine in our intoxication. The actual world itself is thus the most eloquent evidence of dependent origination. The process of interaction – the signature, so to speak, of dependent origination – means that there is always a measure of continuity between past, present and future, but, at the same time, there is also constant change: nothing is reduplicated or remains static.

Recognising dependent origination allows us to see the world as it really is: as a process which is continually flowing. Nothing remains the same, but no utterly discrete new entities ever arise randomly. Everything that arises is part of the flow of dependent origination.

In other words, whatever arises does so through dependence upon causes and conditions. Each and every phenomenon is a contingent phenomenon. Nothing stands alone; nothing exists in itself or by itself, but only comes into being through dependence upon the interaction of causes and conditions, in dependence upon an assemblage of parts and in dependence upon mere imputation.

Right now, our view of the world has been shaped by countless prior lifetimes of erroneous perception, and we are far from intuiting dependent origination. Instead, we imagine that the world is comprised entirely of solid, independent, discrete entities, among which our personal 'self' is the most precious, solid and discrete entity of all. Thus we regard ourselves as unique individuals, with an entirely self-enclosed existence, reliant upon nothing except itself. We imagine in this way that our identity is that of a singular, autonomous and permanent self. We look out on the world, on seemingly external phenomena, whether sentient beings or inanimate things, and see them likewise as discrete, self-reliant, self-existent phenomena, each existing in their own separate spaces. It is as if the world is made up of a multiplicity of individual boxes – some marked 'selves' and some marked 'things'.

Tragically, this denial of the interdependent nature of phenomena has severe consequences. As a result of imagining that our personal self is a self-contained, self-existent, independent entity, we experience fear, loneliness and isolation. Sometimes it is disguised, sometimes obvious. Yet, however hard we try, we cannot quite convince ourselves that we truly possess such a solid identity. Therefore, when we look out anxiously on the world, where we perceive all those seemingly self-existent entities of people and things, we feel compelled to enhance our security. We seek to grasp and appropriate the things which appear attractive and therefore seem to promise a reinforcement of our fragile identity. At the same time, we experience fear towards the other part of the world which does not seem to offer us such security but only an unsettling challenge. In this way, the emotion of hatred arises, which impels us to attack and eliminate everything that seems to threaten us.

Stimulated by these disturbing emotions, we try to act to control the world, to take from it that which we imagine will make us feel secure, and to deny and destroy that which makes us fearful. Hence, our actions (known in Sanskrit as 'karma') are driven by our disturbing emotions. Yet, as we fight with the world in this way, we come only again and again to disappointment, frustration and grief, since none of these entities that we appropriate or destroy ever make us feel secure, because none of them has the character of independence and permanence that we project upon them. In fact, they are all themselves dependently arising phenomena, part of a temporal process and part of a network of interacting circumstances. Their existence is merely contingent, derived from the nexus of causes and conditions from which they emerge.

Consequently, however much we try, we cannot ever succeed in abstracting anything from the world in the way that would be possible if the thing we desired really existed in itself. Whatever we grasp at is always part of a net of interconnections. Our attempts to grasp things to create a sense of security are as futile as trying to build something solid out of a river: a stream of water is merely a process and thus we cannot build anything stable or unchanging out of it. Such is our Sisyphean struggle with the world, rolling our boulder up a hill only to watch it come rolling back down again. This struggle is the root of our tragedy and suffering. The only way to happiness and freedom from suffering is to understand dependent origination. Only this understanding will bring an end to our clinging to an illusory solidity that we foolishly imagine to exist in the world.

The teaching of dependent origination is so profound and subtle that Buddha himself presented it in a number of ways to meet the varying levels of understanding possessed by his followers. To help distinguish the different presentations, we can group the teachings of the Buddha into two categories: the teachings presented from the perspective of 'conventional truth' and those presented from the perspective of 'ultimate truth'. Dependent origination itself straddles both truths, as will become clear, but it is nevertheless useful to understand the difference between these two truths.

'Conventional truth', according to masters such as Sakya Pandita (1182–1250), denotes how appearances manifest to a mind which does not analyse their status and thus assumes them to be existent. 'Ultimate truth' refers to the non-existence of those apparent entities – a non-existence which is only discovered through analysing their nature.

In brief, one might say therefore that the appearance of things is conventional truth. Their lack of true existence, or their 'emptiness', is ultimate truth.

Dependent origination demonstrates how the appearances that we term 'the world' arise. Thus it explains the conventional apparent truth of things. At the same time, it demonstrates that those apparent entities are devoid of true existence, exactly because they are dependent. Dependent origination is thus the key to understanding both ultimate truth and conventional truth. This relationship of dependent origination to the two truths will be in particularly sharp focus in Chapter 5, when we consider the Madhyamaka viewpoint.

Chapter 2
Outer and Inner Phenomena

The Buddha's teaching that all phenomena originate through dependence sets apart his teaching from all other systems of thought. Buddha's system, through its emphasis on dependent origination, denies the need for any supreme creator god in charge of the world and the destinies of beings. According to Buddha, all phenomena arise simply through the collection of causes and conditions. Thus there is neither an independent agent who brought the world into being or who can interfere with it later if it malfunctions and needs some adjustment.

The teaching of dependent origination has radical implications for how we should behave in the world. Precisely because everything originates through dependent origination, there is always a connection between causes and results. Virtuous actions lead to positive results and non-virtuous actions to suffering. Systems which once relied on a notion of God as the reason to behave morally finally eliminate God and veer into moral nihilism. Followers of these systems tend eventually to conclude that, if there is no God after all, there is no point in behaving morally. By contrast, Buddha's teachings explain that since everything originates through dependent origination, actions have consequences. Thus, despite being non-theistic, Buddha's teachings defend the importance of the ethical life. This is one feature that makes Buddha's teachings so revolutionary and an immense source of wisdom about the necessity for ethical behaviour in our modern times, when it so often seems unclear why we should behave morally, let alone what behaving morally even means.

Outer dependent origination

We can see the play of dependent origination in both 'outer phenomena' and 'inner phenomena'. The term 'outer phenomena', used in this context, essentially means that which is embodied – that is to say, possesses a material and hence non-sentient nature. In Buddha's analysis of the world of 'conditioned phenomena' in the abhidharma, material phenomena are grouped under the heading of the 'aggregate' (Skt. *skandha*) of 'form' (Skt. *rupa*). Together with the non-material mental aggregates of 'sensation', 'perception', 'formations' and 'consciousness', these physical phenomena comprise the 'five aggregates', the totality of conditioned phenomena. Here the term 'conditioned' indicates phenomena whose existence is dependent and which are, consequently, subject to transience.

Buddha's decision to use the term 'aggregate', in his explanations of the phenomena that comprise the world of conditions, is itself reflective of his core dictum that everything is dependently arisen. In other words, what might appear to us as substantial entities are themselves only aggregates or compounds: the grouping-together of things from many parts. There is nothing that is simply as we imagine it to be, a self-existent singular entity.

This aggregate of physical form is itself merely an aggregation of phenomena coming together moment-arily and then disintegrating. In total, it comprises the basic elements of earth (solidity), water (fluidity), fire (temperature) and air (motility) and the senses and their objects, which, with the exception of mental objects such as dream images, meditative forms and the 'sub-stance' of vows, derive from those self-same elements.

When we examine the aggregate of *form* more closely, we can see that every material object arises through the interaction of causes and conditions. For instance, a flower only arises through the interaction of its chief cause, the seed, with the appropriate conditions – soil, water, sunlight and so on. Out of the interaction of those causes and conditions emerges the dependently originated phenomenon that we call 'a flower'.

This process does not need an external agent to direct it; no act of will has determined this should hap-pen. To continue the example of the seed, the seed itself does not have the determination to become a flower. However, when the seed interacts with the appropriate conditions, a flower manifests. The seed did not have the thought: 'I must become a flower', and no external agent had such an intention either. It is a purely natu-ral process. We must also understand that the seed itself alone doesn't have the power to establish the flower. An unassisted solitary cause cannot create anything.

From the explanations above, we should now be able to perceive dependent origination a little more clearly. To assert that things are dependently originated is not to imply that a singular thing is the cause of a singular result. Instead, it is to say that phenomena arise out of the *interaction* of causes and conditions. If even only one of these causes and conditions is missing, the resultant phenomenon will not arise.

This analysis of causation is radically different from the analysis invoked by theists who argue that, since there is a world, there must therefore be a creator. One solitary cause cannot produce a single effect. All effects arise in dependence upon the interactions of causes and conditions. This fact makes our analysis of cause and effect much subtler than it might otherwise be. With this understanding, we are thus more cautious in determining something as the cause of something else, as we cannot point to one single cause which gives rise to one single effect.

This perspective on dependent origination is similar to the way people typically think and act in practical matters. If we consider the example of a farmer who is skilled in agriculture, for instance, it is evident that he is well aware that a certain crop only grows from the interaction of causes and conditions. His very livelihood depends upon such knowledge. He knows that the mere possession of barley seeds alone, without the other necessary conditions, will not ensure that he has a barley crop. The barley seed must meet the supporting conditions of good soil, water, sunlight, and so on. This 'common-sense view', so to speak, of the farmer, thus accords with dependent origination.

The example of the seed shows that understanding dependent origination renders our sense of the way that

the world works both very uncluttered and very prag-
matic. We don't need to invent imaginary entities such
as gods to direct things and make the world function.
We begin to see that things come about as a result of a
multiplicity of causes and conditions coming together:
not external entities or random chance. We might say
that the view of dependent origination is thus like a
razor which eliminates the use of unnecessary entities
in explaining how the world works.

Inner dependent origination

The explanation to this point has described outer
dependent origination. The term 'inner dependent
origination' refers to inner or mental phenomena,
which, together with the various 'non-associated' factors
such as acquisition and sequence that form part of the
fourth aggregate, are represented by the aggregates of
sensations, perceptions, formations and consciousness.

According to Buddha, the evolution of phenomena such as happiness and suffering, and even our con-
tinuance in the cycle of birth and death, can be traced
through the twelve dependently originated links (Skt.
nidana) of inner dependent origination, which are as
follows:

1. Ignorance
2. Karmic formations
3. Consciousness
4. Name and form
5. The six sense-bases
6. Contact
7. Sensation

8. Craving
9. Clinging
10. Becoming
11. Birth
12. Old age and death

Just as outer phenomena arise and pass away without the involvement of any creator or directing agent, so too the twelve links, which comprise our experience of the cycle of birth and death, have arisen without any external creator. Since that is the case, their cessation (in the experience of nirvana) likewise will not be dependent on any external agent, such as a divine being, but simply upon our development of the wisdom that sees things as they truly are and thus cuts through the fiction that supports samsara.

As explained in Chapter 1, the cycle of the twelve links of dependent origination arises out of our fundamental misunderstanding of the nature of reality. This misunderstanding is known as the 'obscuration of cognition', which, together with the 'obscuration of disturbing emotions', is one of the two veils, or obscurations, which prevent us from achieving buddhahood.

The obscuration of cognition is, in essence, the dualistic perception that the true nature of reality can be resolved as being either existence or non-existence. In actuality, the true nature is beyond all elaboration by conceptual activity and designation and therefore cannot be placed in any extreme whatsoever. In other words, the obscuration of cognition consists of the fundamental dualistic mistake that we make about the world. It is this mistake which underlies the development of the disturbing emotions, actions and suffering, that together comprise the twelve links.

As Gorampa Sonam Sengge says in defining and distinguishing these two obscurations:

> It appears that both the protector Maitreya and the master Nagarjuna have the same understanding in accepting that the apprehension of phenomena as truly existent is a cognitive obscuration.[3]

And:

> Although the apprehension of 'true existence' which apprehends true existence is a cognitive obscuration, it was described by Aryadeva as the seed of samsara, because it generates ignorance, one of the twelve links.[4]

In other words, a distinction must be drawn between (i) the subtle ignorance that constitutes the cognitive obscuration and (ii) the ignorance that is a part of the obscuration of disturbing emotions. The former is the cause of the twelve links themselves. The latter is merely the first of the twelve links. In any case, until the obscurations produced by the disturbing emotions and the cognitive obscuration are dissolved by primordial wisdom, the wheel of the twelve links will continue to turn, resting, as it does, upon the basis of the subtler obscuration itself.

Chapter 3
The Twelve Links

The succession of the twelve links of dependent origination resembles the revolving of a wheel: each link is the necessary condition for the next. Although the links seem to start with the link of ignorance, the twelfth link of dependent origination (old age and death) is in fact also the necessary condition for the arising of ignorance (the first link). It is for this reason that there seems to be a repetitive element to our experience. We should not mistake this repetitive element for some sort of notion of an 'eternal return' in which things are always precisely the same every time around, but, nevertheless, there is a kind of circularity to experience in samsara. As we keep proceeding through these cycles in which each of the links follow in sequence, similar types of experience occur, and each cycle acts as the foundation for the next. In the cycle of births and deaths, we thus are strapped to a wheel made up of the twelve links.

In their most obvious manifestation, the twelve links of dependent origination play out over three lifetimes: the preceding life, the present life and the future life.

As Jamgon Ju Mipham says:

> If one examines how many lives it takes to complete a cycle of twelve links, it is taught that they are completed within the three lifetimes of the previous, the present and the future.[5]

However, in addition to this time-frame, the twelve links can even be completed in a very brief span of time.

Again, as Jamgon Ju Mipham states:

> There is a manner in which the twelve links are contained within the moment of completing an act.[6]

There is no contradiction here: it is just the understanding that smaller cycles are operating within larger cycles – such as many cycles of a day, a week, an hour, or even a moment, operating within longer cycles such as a lifetime, three lifetimes or longer.

With this understanding of such complementary but different temporal frameworks, we should examine the individual links.

1. Ignorance

Ignorance, as the first of the twelve links, is the disturbing emotion which attributes a self – permanent, singular and autonomous – to one or more of the aggregates. In fact, when we examine the aggregates one by one or

as a whole, we find that they are multiple, impermanent, impure and selfless. We might object that, if that is
correct, ignorance would then be something that only
a philosopher capable of articulating such concepts as
'self' could suffer. Yet we are not referring merely to
the description of the concepts: it is the deep-rooted
emotional attachment that we possess, regardless of
whether or not we can articulate or explain it. All sentient beings, except buddhas, manifest this ignorance
because all cling to the sense of self. We don't need to be
able to articulate this in a philosophical way: as long as
we have the emotional attachment to the notion of 'I' or
'mine', we are afflicted by this form of ignorance.

2. Karmic formations

As is said: 'On the basis of ignorance, there arise karmic
formations.'

Due to this ignorance that grasps at the mere 'I', our
basic outlook is inevitably self-centred. Consequently,
we are driven to defend and aggrandise this self at all
times. In such a way, the ground for the way we act in
the world through our body, speech and mind is established. Our actions, conditioned by ignorance, become
habitual patterns of behaviour which, in turn, influence
our way of relating to the world. So, this karmic pattern-
ing, or 'karmic formations', drives us forward.

3. Consciousness

As is said: 'On the basis of karmic formations there
arises consciousness.'

These links evolve over a series of lifetimes. The first two links – ignorance and karmic formations – relate to the previous life. At the stage of the link of consciousness, this is the moment at which a new life is about to begin.

What exactly is meant by the statement: 'On the basis of karmic formations arises consciousness'?

The answer is that the actions that we have performed shape our attitudes. These actions create imprints that travel forward in the continuum of mind. In such a fashion, our consciousness is karmically contaminated by the imprints of past actions. That 'contaminated' consciousness will itself act as the foundation for the subsequent links.

This consciousness is thus an impelled consciousness. It is driven forward by karmic contaminations and the ignorance which is the basis for those karmic formations. It is those two preceding links which cause the linking consciousness to be driven on to rebirth.

This third link thus joins the past life with the present life. However, it is not a present life that it chooses freely, since, as just explained, consciousness is impelled by the karmic formations. Neither is it the case that there is some external agent, such as a God, which commands the linking consciousness: 'You should go there!' Neither is it a consciousness that suddenly pops into existence from nothingness. What is more, it is certainly not a consciousness that is a 'blank slate' devoid of any content, since it is contaminated by karmic formations and ignorance.

4. Name and form

Regarding the fourth link, it is said: 'On the basis of consciousness there is name and form.'

'Name and form' is simply another way to designate the five aggregates, which are none other than the physical and the mental basis upon which one will project the notion of a self. 'Name' designates the four mental aggregates: sensations, perceptions, formations and consciousness. 'Form' is the first aggregate.

These two links of 'consciousness' and 'name and form' represent the juncture point where the interaction between inner and outer phenomena occurs. Specifically, the impelled consciousness, now driven by karmic formations and ignorance, enters into the physical world. In the case of a human birth, consciousness enters into a human life. The consciousness is mixed together with the male and female elements from the parents at the moment of conception and thus 'name' and 'form' come together.

Therefore the process of 'name and form' is actually two interacting processes of dependent origination coming together. The first process is the consciousness that enters the physical world from the intermediate state between death and rebirth. Consciousness is dependently originated from the preceding links of ignorance and karmic formations. The second process is the physical form, which is dependently originated from the male and female drops. We should notice that the male and female physical elements which are present at conception do not constitute the necessary dependent connections for the consciousness ('name') that joins them to create 'name and form', because the physical elements ('form') are merely material and not endowed with sentience. In other words, the consciousness part of 'name and form' can only arise in dependence upon the prior moment of consciousness, which was that of the 'intermediate state'.

Name and form, like the third link (consciousness) and the six sense-bases (the fifth link), contact (the sixth link), sensations (the seventh link), birth (the eleventh link) and old age and death (the twelfth link) belongs to the group of links known collectively as 'suffering'. Ignorance (the first link), craving and clinging (the eighth and ninth links) form the group of 'disturbing emotions'. Karmic formations (the second link) and becoming (the tenth link) constitute the group of 'karma', because they are creative actions. The links that embody suffering are, in a way, resultant, as they come about through the influence of the disturbing emotions and karma.

To be more precise about this fourth link – under the influence of the karmic formations which have impelled the consciousness, the consciousness of a being in the intermediate state (that is, the period between one life and the next), will be attracted to karmically appropriate parents. Those who, due to karmic conditioning, are to be genetically male will be attracted to the female element represented by the mother and will have a repulsion to the male element represented by the father, and vice versa. This again shows how the 'name and form' link is itself a dependently originated phenomenon.

The karmic contaminations impelling the consciousness are also a cause for that consciousness to link itself with the appropriate world from amongst the six realms. If virtuous karmic imprints are ripening at that time, the consciousness would be attracted to the human realm and, therefore, would be conceived as a human being.

5. The six sense-bases

As is said: 'On the basis of name and form there arise the six sense-bases.'

As the newly conceived being matures in the womb, the sense faculties through which consciousness beholds the apparently external world begin to develop. These six senses might be described as 'six windows looking onto the world': a world initially restricted to the interior of the mother's body and then, following birth, comprising that which is external.

6. Contact

As is said: 'On the basis of the six senses arises contact.'

Contact is the link that denotes the joining together of the perceiving senses with the apparently external world.

7. Sensations

As is said: 'On the basis of contact arises the link of sensations.'

The consciousness that apprehends things through the doors of the six senses is karmically biased towards preferring some experiences and rejecting others. It is for this reason that the links from consciousness through to and including sensations are considered to be 'resultant' links.

Consequently, when the perceiving mind meets the external world, it assigns it into three distinct categories: those which it finds pleasant, those which it finds unpleasant and those to which it is indifferent.

8. Craving

As is said: 'On the basis of sensations arise craving.'

'Craving', in this context, is the desire to repeat a pleasant experience that arose out of 'contact' or, equally, the determination to avoid an unpleasant one. We might say that in this link the apprehending consciousness is becoming more involved with its objects and more defined by them.

9. Clinging

As is said: 'On the basis of craving there is clinging.'

'Clinging' is an intensification of the reaction to the world that was manifesting in craving. It is the formation of a kind of fixation or dependency, as we are now driven by a strong compulsion to possess the object.

10. Becoming

As is said: 'On the basis of clinging, there arises becoming.'

At the link of becoming, we are moving towards the future life. Unless interrupted, the clinging which constituted the preceding link creates a kind of habitual way of responding to the world. This set of habits, in turn, forms the kind of person we will be and hence this link is termed 'becoming'. It is this 'build up' of a profoundly felt sense of solidity which will push us to the next life.

Thus, the links running from sensation to becoming delineate the stages in the process of the establishment of what we might describe as 'identity'. Due to habits from the past, we respond to certain experiences in particular ways. If those experiences – such as the experience of pleasure from a certain type of object – are very strong, we start to become dependent on them. We search for them and we build our activities and our life around them. Gradually, we begin to be shaped by those objects and experiences. Our identity, as represented in the link of becoming, is thus itself a dependently originated phenomenon.

Incidentally, one should realise that there is an almost limitless number of objects, whether it be physical or mental, around which we might develop an identity. Thus, in addition to crude physical preferences towards particular physical objects or people, it might be aesthetic tastes, intellectual opinions or ideological convictions, developed in dependence upon responses and habit, that cause us to develop an identity and worldview, both of which come to feel like an objective reality. However, in fact, they have come into being in dependence upon the repeated movement of the wheel of the twelve links.

By the time we reach this link of 'becoming', we feel a certain solidity in our identity and views such that we might think: 'I am just what I am, that's it! I know I'm real! I feel I'm real! Whatever you want to call it, there's no mistake about what I am! That's the way the world is, that's the way I am!' It is a heavy, solid feeling. It could concern our ideological position; it could be a way we relate to sensual pleasure. All of these habits have built up to such a point that they feel inevitable and solid through this process.

In this way, the links move forward like a flood, each link giving rise to the next, giving rise to the next in turn, endlessly and so swiftly that we don't notice the process.

11. Birth

As is said: 'On the basis of becoming, there arises birth.'

'Birth' refers to the moment of arising in the next life. Of course, how we arise in the next life is impelled by what we have become through the sequence of the preceding links.

12. Old age and death

As is said: 'On the basis of birth, there arise ageing, sickness, death, sorrow, lamentation – in short, suffering.'

What follows inevitably from having re-entered embodiment through the process of conception and birth is 'old age, sickness and death' – which, together with birth itself, are known as 'the four rivers of suffering'.

Alongside the inescapable consequence of being driven into rebirth once more, we must experience the manifold sufferings of separation from loved ones, meeting with those to whom one is averse, the inability to acquire that which one desires and the sorrow of losing what one has.

As Nagarjuna says:

> When there is birth there is affliction, sickness and
> ageing,
> Deprivation, death, fear and so forth.
> The extremely great heap of these sufferings will arise.[7]

That twelfth link is then succeeded by ignorance, in the first of a new cycle. In such a way, the wheel continues to turn, unless the wisdom that recognises the true nature of reality supervenes.

As we noted above, in addition to the sequence of twelve links that might occur over a series of lifetimes, the process can also operate during the course of one lifetime or within an ever-briefer timeframe. In this sense, there are long-term cycles of dependent origination over a number of lifetimes and smaller cycles playing out within them.

In this way, without knowing it, we bring to our present experience the ignorance and the karmic formations from the past. When we experience certain objects, feelings of pleasure or displeasure arise, that harden into a kind of craving and finally into a dependency. We become deeply involved with that object, really involved with experiencing it until it dominates us completely. We totally fixate upon that object and our whole identity is shaped by it. Then, of course, the experience breaks up, and we look for another experience, another object, which then shapes our identity for the future.

All this means that no experience that we have is free and unconditioned, until we have uprooted the twelve links, because, wherever we might go or seek to hide, we bring this karmic legacy, this impetus from the past, to each and every fresh experience. That's why we cannot relate to any experience in an undistorted way until this wheel is stopped, which, as we saw in Chapter 1, can only come about through developing wisdom and uprooting ignorance.

One might say that this explanation of dependent origination as it relates to 'inner phenomena' is actually an extended commentary on the second Noble Truth, the cause of suffering. In this process, one link gives rise to the next, which gives rise to the next. Unless we deliberately introduce a pause, there is no space or gap between the links. One link just gives rise to the other without end.

By examining the dependent origination of 'outer phenomena', we can develop an intelligence about how the physical world seems to work. Similarly, by recognising the process of development embodied in these twelve links, we can start to develop an intelligence about what has shaped our perceptions, habits and experience: about how past lives have shaped this life and how this life shapes future lives.

This explanation of dependent origination of outer and inner phenomena might lead us to assume that reality comprises the two separate categories of the physical and the mental, each having their own types of dependent origination, as thinkers of the Vaibhashika and Sautrantika philosophical systems of Buddhism maintained. However, when we look at the Mahayana presentation of dependent origination in the next two chapters, any such dualistic picture will dissolve and we will see that physical and mental are not separate as we might imagine.

Chapter 4
The Chittamatra Perspective

The Chittamatra tenet system is a philosophical school of Buddhism that was developed by Asanga and Vasubandhu in India in the fourth century BCE on the basis of the sutras of the Third Turning of the Wheel given by the Buddha. The Sanskrit word 'Chittamatra' describes its key philosophical view: Mind-Only, which reflects the statement made by Buddha in the *Dasabhumika Sutra*:

The three realms are only mind, sons of the Conqueror.[8]

A major influence on this system was provided by the bodhisattva Maitreya's direct teachings in such texts as the *Madhyantavibhaga*, in which he expounded the teaching of 'the three natures': the 'imaginary', the 'dependent' and the 'completely established'. Maitreya's analysis of perception and experience reveals how we construct the world in different ways according to conceptual activity or 'false imagination'. In this respect, our present view that the world comprises truly existent selves and intrinsically existent objects is no more than deluded conceptualisation that projects its errors onto the world of experience and thus creates a fictitious structure through which we misread reality.

Since this world of 'true selves' and 'true objects' is completely unreal and non-existent, it is known as the 'imaginary nature'. This deluded perception rests upon mind itself, in that the imagined objects and subjects are merely its projections, the activity of its 'false imagination'. However, in the Chittamatra system, the actual nature of such projections is termed the 'dependent nature', indicating that both subject and object are mutually dependent and rest upon mind, hence the expression 'Mind-Only'.

According to the Chittamatra system, mind itself is therefore existent, unlike its projections, which, as we have noted, are merely the imagined entities that comprise the 'imaginary nature'. Although mind is existent, in that without mind there would not be anything at all, it is empty in the sense of being devoid of the duality of subject and object. This mode of emptiness is termed the third nature – 'the thoroughly established nature' – because it is the absolutely real.

As Maitreya states:

> This also is the imaginary, the dependent
> And the thoroughly established.
> These are taught with reference to objects,
> The false imagination, and the absence of the two.[9]

As all phenomena are nothing more than mind, both the suffering of samsara and the bliss of nirvana have no other origin than mind. To explain how these phenomena are dependently originated from mind, Chittamatrin thinkers delineate eight consciousness groups, comprising (i) the all-ground consciousness, the basis from which the sense-consciousnesses arise, and (ii) the egoic consciousness (Skt. *manas*), thus adding two (the manas and the all-ground consciousness) to the usual depiction of consciousness as six-fold.

As Karmapa Rangjung Dorje says:

> All of samsara and nirvana are mind only.
> The six consciousnesses, the manas and the all-ground consciousness
> Are explained as their dependently originated causes and conditions.[10]

Since there is nothing external to mind, the entire cycle (one might say 'history') of samsara, as depicted in the twelve links of dependent origination, takes place within the 'false imagination', which is just the activity of mind. As long as the 'manas' (the obscured, egoic consciousness) grasps at the all-ground consciousness as a 'self' and grasps at the appearances that arise through the six senses as its objects, then disturbing emotions, karma and suffering will follow.

The Chittamatra teaching that there is nothing which is truly existent external to mind may be understood through reasoning and analogy. For instance, one can establish that all perceptible objects are dependent on the perceiving consciousness, and that there is not something 'out there' that can be perceived 'as it really is', by considering how a glass of water appears in different ways to beings in different realms. In this respect, for a human in good health, there appears to be the manifest appearance of water, but for the gods, there is the manifest appearance of nectar; for a hell being, there is the manifest appearance of the weapons of hell; a fish sees the water as home; and a human being with jaundice sees it as yellow; a human being with rabies sees it as poison; and so on. Each of these seeming objects of perception are merely dependently arising appearances; they possess no more reality than that. The analogy, incidentally, does not indicate that there is any commonality to the imprints operative in the beings from different realms, nor that there is some actually hidden common object which is merely misconstrued by the perceiving agent. So, finally, it would be most accurate to say: 'hell beings see weapons' and 'human beings see water'.

It is not that the perceiving mind is misinterpreting some real object which is out there somewhere. Continuing the example above, there is no truly existent glass of water that can be perceived 'as it really is'. Even though objects appear vividly, clearly and in an unobstructed way to the perceiving consciousness, the objects are nothing other than the mind: the consciousness itself. The perceiving consciousness itself is also a dependent phenomenon, because if there is no truly existent external object being referred to in this experience, there is no truly existent subject perceiving it either: there can be no subject without an object. As the object is dependent, so must the subject be, and, thus, the error of solipsism is avoided – that is, the error of thinking that 'everything is really just me', that it is all *my* mind, and that 'I' (unlike everyone else) see things validly.

If there were truly existent external objects and a truly existent inner perceiver, contact between them would not be possible, since, if they both existed in their own separate space (as such truly existent entities must necessarily do) they would never meet. As a consequence, there would be no perception arising in such a case.

One may also understand this by considering examples such as dreams. At night one goes to sleep and vivid images arise, which we take to be truly existent entities external to us and therefore we react to them with a feeling of pleasure or displeasure – in other words, with craving. Various actions seem to happen in the dream in dependence upon those apparently existent objects. Yet, when we awaken, we realise the objects and actions were never really existent in the first place: all this was just the dependently originated activity of mind.

The objects appearing in the dream and the sense of self as the perceiver of those objects are both just mind. Indeed, we cannot even identify an essential difference between experience now while we are awake, and that experience in dreams. Whatever particular dream occurs does not depend upon external objects and an inner perceiver, but merely comes about through the ripening of imprints. In the same way, the events of this life, taking the guise of physical objects and inner perceivers, are also simply the ripening of karmic imprints in the stream of mind. The only difference is in the relative strength of the karmic imprints: the imprints producing daytime appearances are usually stronger than those giving rise to dream experience.

Thus the answer to the question of how the mind interacts with the physical world – the question of how the dependently originated 'inner phenomena' connect with the dependently originated 'outer phenomena' – is, in fact, that there are no outer phenomena separate from inner phenomena. Both are, according to the Mind-Only system, simply mind, and the variety of appearances that arise are the ripening of imprints within mind.

Chapter 5
The Madhyamaka Perspective

The Madhyamaka system of tenets was elaborated originally by Nagarjuna and Aryadeva in the first and second centuries CE, on the basis of the sutras taught by the Buddha in 'The Second Turning of the Wheel'. This system was later extended by such masters as Bhavya, Chandrakirti, Shantideva and Shantarakshita between the sixth and eighth centuries. The Sanskrit word Madhyamaka means 'Middle Way', and these two terms are used interchangeably to refer to this system.

In the view of the masters of the Madhyamaka, the presentations of dependent origination by the Vaibhashikas, Sautrantikas and Chittamatrins were somewhat deficient, as Madhyamaka thinkers considered that these other systems still tended to affirm a kind of subtle intrinsic nature (whether truly existent moments of mind or truly existent irreducible particles). The Madhyamaka thinkers, by contrast, upheld that whatever is dependently originated must be empty of intrinsic nature, because if an entity had an intrinsic nature, or true existence, its existence would not be dependent on anything whatsoever: it would exist in itself.

Simply put, the view of the Madhyamaka is that all these other systems, in maintaining a subtle 'existence' view, do not represent the Middle Way view which transcends all conceptual positions about reality. By contrast, in the authentic Middle Way view, dependent origination and emptiness are understood as one reality, and, consequently, all extreme views of existence and non-existence, eternalism and annihilationism are transcended.

The Madhyamaka refutation of Vaibhashika and Sautrantika

There are some very subtle distinctions between the Vaibhashika and Sautrantika systems, which are outside the scope of the present work. For the purpose of this overview, however, it makes sense to treat them together as representative of the general Shravakayana view. It might also be useful to cast the Madhyamaka critique of this view in the form of a dialogue in which the Madhyamika will employ a so-called 'argument by consequence' (Skt. *prasanga*) to expose the contradiction within his opponent's views. This dialogue form is used to great effect in many major ancient Indian, and subsequently Tibetan, philosophical works and commentaries.

As the dialogue begins, the Shravaka has just asserted that momentary phenomena, whether irreducible particles of matter or instants of consciousness truly exist.

MADHYAMIKA: You claim that momentary phenomena truly exist. If this is so, how do these momentary existent atoms and minds originate?

SHRAVAKA: They originate by dependent origination, of course!

MADHYAMIKA: Are you sure you really believe that? Is it your position that in one moment there are particles manifesting which then cease, after which another set of particles arise, endure momentarily and likewise cease, after which yet another set of particles arise, endure and cease?

SHRAVAKA: Yes, that is what we think.

MADHYAMIKA: So are you saying that particle A exists now, then ceases and after that particle B arises?

SHRAVAKA: Yes, that is an accurate description of our position.

MADHYAMIKA: But how can particle B be dependently arisen from particle A?

SHRAVAKA: What do you mean?

MADHYAMIKA: Your answer makes no sense at all. Look carefully and ask yourself this question: 'Has particle A ceased when particle B arises or is it still existent?'

The Shravaka stays silent at this point. He now sees the problem with his argument. If he were to claim that particle A is still existent at the time particle B arises, he would, in fact, be asserting that the cause (particle A) and the effect (particle B) exist in the same moment, which is not possible. If he were to make this claim, it would be the same as if he were to assert that the seed and the shoot exist at the same time. The Shravaka at this stage tries one final line of argument in response to the Madhyamika's question.

> SHRAVAKA: Particle B arises after Particle A has ceased.

> MADHYAMIKA: The consequence of your claim is that particle B would be arising from nothing, since there would be a gap – a space – that is left immediately following the cessation of particle A. In this case, there would be absolutely no connection between particle B and particle A, so how can you say that particle B is the fruit of particle A?

The Shravaka has no way of explaining how his postulated intrinsically existent entities could originate. The same problem exists with his account of inner phenomena, that is, the mind itself. According to the Vaibhashika and Sautrantika systems, consciousness is no unchanging self, but it does consist of truly existent moments of consciousness. Saying that something is truly existent signifies that it must exist separately from other phenomena. However, this assertion runs into the same difficulty as their assertions about the physical world.

For the Vaibhashikas and Sautrantikas, a moment of consciousness arises, endures for an instant and then ceases. It is then succeeded by the next entirely distinct moment of consciousness. Once again, the Vaibhashikas and Sautrantikas cannot successfully defend this mode of origination, because in asserting this, they are, in fact, claiming that the second moment of consciousness must have arisen without a cause, since there must be a gap that would have to exist between one moment of consciousness and the next entirely distinct moment of consciousness. In such a case there would be no continuum of consciousness and no causative relationship between the two moments of consciousness because they would be entirely unconnected.

However, if, to overcome that problem, they were to claim that there is no such gap between the two moments of consciousness, those two moments would have to occupy the very same moment in time. In such a case, the first moment of consciousness, which is the cause, and the subsequent moment of consciousness, which is the fruit, would both have to exist in the same moment. The problem with this argument is that cause and fruit cannot exist simultaneously, just as a seed and its imputed fruit cannot exist at the same time.

The Madhyamaka view is thus that phenomena clearly do arise, but they are dependently originated phenomena lacking any intrinsic nature. For instance, barley shoots arise from barley seeds that are present together with the right conditions such as water, soil and sunlight. In this case, the cause (barley seed) and fruit (barley shoot) are neither identical, which they would be if they existed in the same moment, nor radically distinct, in separate moments. In fact, if one intrinsically existent entity could be the cause of another entirely distinct entity, rice seeds could be the cause of barley shoots.

Similarly, as we saw earlier, if we examine the process of dependent origination at work in rebirth, we can see that, whilst the physical aspect of the fourth link, 'name and form', is derived from physical elements constituted by the male and female elements of the parents, the mind aspect is derived from the linking consciousness that is the third of the twelve links. Thus the 'result' – the consciousness of the newly conceived being – is neither the same nor different from its 'cause', the linking consciousness. Thus cause and effect are not of a totally dissimilar nature, since, if that were the case, anything could arise at random from anything.

As Chandrakirti says:

> If another is produced from another, then even from
>   flames could come darkness.
> From any cause, any fruit could arise,
> But all cause and fruit are similar.
> That which can be produced is termed 'fruit'.
> That which can produce that, though different, is
>   termed 'cause'.
> The cause and fruit belong to the same continuum.[11]

Thus there is always a dependent connection between causes and effects, expressed by Buddha in the phrase: 'This existing, that arises.'

The world therefore works through dependent origination, but, as we have now seen, the Shravaka description of dependent origination is incompatible with its actual reality, since it still affirms the existence of entities that, in the final analysis, don't exist.

We cannot find any truly existent entity in the world. If there were one, then the world would cease to exist, because there could be no change, no development, no growth, and no interaction. It is precisely this change, development, growth, impermanence and interaction that characterises the world. So radical is this teaching that we might, at some level, fear losing the world if we were to realise that the world is not how we imagine it to be. In fact, we should not fear that if things were empty there would be no world, because, contrary to what we might mistakenly assume, it is emptiness alone that makes the world possible. This is because 'emptiness' is just another word for the dependent origination through which all the phenomena that we term 'the world' come into being.

As Chandrakirti explains:

> Even though all things are empty,
> From empty causes and conditions they clearly arise.
> As they have no intrinsic nature in either of the two
>   truths
> They are neither permanent nor subject to annihilation.[12]

In mistakenly asserting or thinking that phenomena possess intrinsic nature, we are projecting onto the world the notion that there are hard borders marking one thing off from another. However, if there were such discrete boundaries in time and in space, nothing could ever arise, because things would be arising from nothingness, which is, of course, impossible. So, even though the Shravaka view is much subtler than any non-Buddhist view in that it accepts the non-existence of the self attributed to the individual, it is limited in its profundity because it attempts to retain the idea of discrete boundaries between phenomena.

In fact, provided that one does not take it as representing ultimate truth, the Shravaka way of talking about causation is very useful in understanding how the world works. While it is not a complete view, because it takes the momentary phenomena designated as 'cause' and 'effect' as being truly existent (which, according to the Madhyamaka is, finally, not the ultimate view), it does nevertheless provide a logical basis for taking actions and their results seriously, without falling into the trap of the entirely erroneous idea of truly existent permanent 'selves' (or a creator God) that is postulated in eternalist thinking that similarly emphasise moral be-haviour.

The Madhyamaka Refutation of Chittamatra

A similar method of reasoning can be used to refute the Chittamatra position. Unlike the Shravakas, who assert that there are truly existent moments, the non-dual view of the Chittamatra school allows it to reduce the number of phenomena that is asserted to be truly exist-ent, but the Chittamatrins nevertheless assert that one phenomenon *does* remain truly existent: the mind it-self. For the Chittamatrin, the truly existent mind, the basis of all, is a continuum made up of irreducible – and hence truly existent – moments of consciousness.

Consequently, the Chittamatra position cannot withstand the Madhyamaka analysis that was used earlier to unpick the Shravaka theory of a mental con-tinuum. Chittamatra, in its assertion of the truly exist-ent continuum of consciousness, has the same problem as the Shravakas in explaining the origination of each moment of mind in this continuum. The mind of the succeeding moment cannot exist at the same time as the mind of the preceding moment, nor can it arise from the gap that would exist if each moment were a discrete self-contained and self-existent moment of mind. Thus, in the absence of any coherent account of the possible origination of such a mind, it is necessary to abandon any claim that there is a truly existent, albeit moment-ary, mind.

Therefore even the non-dual mind proposed by Chittamatra as ultimately real cannot be found. With that understanding, there is no phenomenon left to which one can attach the label 'truly existent', whether it is the eight consciousness groups asserted by Chitta-matra, the five aggregates of the Shravakas or the indi-vidual self of the non-Buddhists.

As Chandrakirti declared:

> Teachings in which it is said that 'the all-ground exists'
> 'The individual exists' and 'the five aggregates exist'
> Are for those who do not understand
> The more profound meaning.[13]

Establishing the Correct Understanding of Dependent Origination

Despite the superiority of the Madhyamaka view in pointing to the ultimate truth of things, the Chitta-matra approach is a very useful way to establish conven-tional truth, since it offers a very subtle description of the manner in which the particular appearances of the world arise for us due to the ripening of karmic imprints in the all-ground consciousness.

By employing these instructions from Chittamatra, we can acquire certainty that all appearances are originated in dependence upon mind. When certainty has arisen, we should then follow the Madhyamaka in analysing the mind itself: is it a truly existent phenomenon that possesses intrinsic nature, or is this mental experience itself also dependently originated?

When we consider the variety of appearances, we come to understand that they arise due to the gathering of particular causes and conditions: appearances do not arise spontaneously. More specifically, those causes and conditions of appearance are the karmic imprints. When appropriate imprints ripen, particular appearances manifest. When those imprints are not present, those particular appearances will not manifest.

However, that would not be the case if mind had an intrinsic nature, because mind would then determine whatever appearances arose by itself without reference to any conditions whatsoever. Furthermore, those appearances would always conform to mind's intrinsic nature. For instance, if one takes an object made of a blue material, any part that is cut or broken off it can only be blue, owing to the blueness of the original object. Similarly, if mind had an intrinsic nature of a certain type, then everything would be in conformity with that, just as objects that derive from the blue object possesses 'blueness'.

Thus mind has no intrinsic nature, and it simply reflects whatever the causes and conditions that are present at that time. What we think of as 'the appearances of mind' are merely dependently arising phenomena, arising through the gathering of particular causes and conditions.

One can consider this by using the example of a magician who creates illusions. Through the combination of his skill, his assistants and his props, the magician causes his audience to behold particular marvels, when, actually, these appearances have no intrinsic nature whatsoever; they merely manifest through the coming together of causes and conditions. Similarly, whatever we see or experience just arises out of the coming together of particular karmic causes and the appropriate conditions.

We might also consider the example of the reflection of the moon in a pool of water. We perceive a clear distinct appearance of the moon in the water, but this is solely because of the gathering together of the appropriate conditions: the satellite of the Earth, a cloudless sky, a pool of water on the ground, and the passing by of a perceiving subject. Out of the interaction of these conditions, the clear distinct appearance of the moon manifests in the water, but it is merely a reflection devoid of any intrinsic nature. The reflection is a dependently originated phenomenon, which has no intrinsic nature of any kind whatsoever. Yet at the same time, it is not merely nothingness: there is a distinct appearance. This is the characteristic of dependently originated phenomena: clearly appearing without any intrinsic nature. One cannot abstract the reflection of the moon from the water, because it does not have a separate existence. In fact, the manifestation of all phenomena is just like that reflection of the moon in the water: they appear, but only through the interaction of causes and conditions. So there is no need to cling to the idea of a truly existent mind as their creator. Mind is, itself, empty of such an intrinsic nature.

There are many other examples we could employ to realise how all phenomena simply arise as illusions: mirages, clouds, lightning, the imaginary palaces that one beholds in the sky in a cloud formation, rainbows, or optical illusions over bodies of water. These things all appear clearly, but without any intrinsic nature, because they merely manifest through dependent origination.

We might at this point object that while we accept that appearances such as the appearance of the moon in water or a rainbow are clearly illusory, the circumstances that create them (such as sunlight and rain in the sky) are actually real phenomena and thus we might still believe that the illusion comes about through real causes and conditions. To believe this would be to misunderstand dependent origination, because we would still be clinging to those causes and conditions themselves as substantially existent.

In order to avoid this error, we should look very precisely at the process of origination and the nature of causes and results. We could consider a further example of a lit candle. We might say that, with this candle, we can light a second candle and thus that the first candle is the cause of the second. Yet, in the case of the light of the candle, if one says that the light of the first candle has ceased, and now a second candle is alight, then there will be nothing for the second one to come from. It cannot be the case that the light of the first candle has ceased to exist, nor did it become the light of the second candle; neither do they exist in the same space, as the cause and effect cannot exist in the same moment of time.

Therefore, although it is relatively true to say that results arise in dependence upon causes, we cannot ultimately isolate any such truly existent entities as 'cause' and 'effect' in this process. There are never truly existent causes to give rise to truly existent effects. Of course, in order to communicate and to be effective in the world, we use conventionally valid language such as saying 'This is the cause of that', but, when we really examine in precise detail the process of origination, causes and results are merely imputed as such. They are dependently originated and, hence, empty phenomena, since a result may only be designated as such in dependence upon a 'cause'. Yet, as we have seen, the two cannot exist simultaneously nor can we truly determine something as a 'result' in the absence of a 'cause'. Nowhere, then, are there any entities which exist with intrinsic nature, and this is true also for the causes and conditions out of which apparent phenomena arise and for the apparent results arising from those apparent causes and conditions.

Dependent origination and compassion

We might wonder how such seemingly high philosophical reasoning relates to the development of compassion. It is clear that what presently obstructs the development of compassion is our clinging to the notion of self – the notion that we now, mistakenly, think can give us a sense of security and solidity but results only in suffering. Our erroneous attachment to self prompts us to perceive the world as if there is a gulf that separates us from all other beings, whom we also imagine to exist in their own self-enclosed spaces. So, conversely, the more we realise how we and others, and indeed the whole world, are dependently originated phenomena and do not possess any such intrinsic nature or permanent, singular and autonomous self, the more space there is for compassion to arise.

If we can develop some understanding of how dependent origination has manifested in our life, this will help to dissolve the rigidity of our sense of self. In fact, the key to developing love to others is nothing other than realising our dependence upon others – a dependence which is incompatible with how we currently view our self – and then developing gratitude towards them. In this respect, it is often very useful to begin by acknowledging one's gratitude to one's parents.

We could then extend that sense of gratitude outwards gradually until we realise how we have been dependent upon the kindness of all sentient beings. In meditating in this manner, we are drawing from a recognition of interdependence to develop the response of loving-kindness and compassion to others.

If we were to consider the history of our life, we would conclude that, in myriad ways, our life is itself a dependently originated phenomenon. For instance, the moment of conception is the union of the bardo consciousness with the male and female elements borrowed from our parents. Our very first moment of existence in this life is utterly dependent upon others and it will proceed like that through the next nine months and then the years of childhood and so on. Thus, until now, one's existence has been contingent upon the kindness of others.

In time, as this sense of interdependence and gratitude to others grows, the strong aspiration that they should be endowed with happiness and its causes, and, equally, be free from suffering and its causes, begins to arise in us. This twin aspiration is none other than the love and kindness that act as the catalysts for the noblest aspiration of all, bodhichitta, the wish to become a buddha for the benefit of others. Thus our entry onto and practice of the Mahayana itself arises in dependence upon our sense of connectedness with others.

Chapter 6
Dependent Origination in the Vajrayana

The Vajrayana is the path that was revealed in the teachings known as the tantras. The term 'tantra' indicates the special understanding that underpins this system. As Lopon Sonam Tsemo says:

> 'Tantra' signifies the continuum of the non-dual mind, existing in an unbroken continuum from time without beginning until buddhahood.[14]

This continuum is the non-dual luminous and empty mind, present in all three phases of the spiritual path: the 'basis' (our state now as ordinary sentient beings), the 'path' itself (as it arises for those with yogic experience) and the 'fruit' (the resultant state experienced by buddhas). In regard to this, one might not see the connection between these three states and might imagine that one's actual nature is radically distinct from that of buddhas and bodhisattvas. Yet that view is erroneous, because, as the tantra teaches, there is no fundamental difference between the nature of the mind of a sentient being and that of a buddha, in that both are the union of luminosity and emptiness. Thus, understood in this way, what arises at buddhahood, the time of the result, arises in dependence upon what is already present in the phases of the basis and the path.

To understand this, we might consider the example of copper. Copper can be utilised to create unattractive things such as drinking bowls for animals or for making beautiful and sacred objects such as statues, but whatever it is used to create, the actual nature of the copper never changes. Similarly, in practising the Vajrayana path, we are not creating some new entity and new qualities that will comprise buddhahood, since these already exist in one's mind: the nature of the mind, just like the copper used to make the different objects in the example, never changes. All that distinguishes a buddha is that he or she has recognised realised this nature, whilst we have not.

According to the great eighth-century master Virupa, dependent origination is the profound key which unlocks the meaning of Vajrayana.

As Konchog Lhundrup declared:

The lord of yogins, Virupa, considered that dependent origination was crucial in the path of Vajrayana.[15]

In fact, as we have seen already in the previous chapters, both samsara and nirvana arise through dependent origination. As regards samsara, it arises on the basis of the three poisonous emotions of desire, hatred and ignorance. Nirvana, by contrast, arises in dependent origination upon the total purification brought about by the path. According to the Vajrayana, if one knows this profound point and possesses the requisite skilful means that comprise the practice of the path, even the disturbing emotions and conceptualisation can be utilised on the path. However, if one does not know this, the profound practices of Vajrayana, such as meditating on deities or emptiness alone, will just become obstacles.

The path itself is established through dependent connections and the root of those connections is to receive initiation. In receiving initiation the necessary dependent connections between the phases of the basis and the fruit are brought about that will allow for the practice of the transformative path. Thus, when a person receives a major initiation in an anuttarayoga mandala, his or her aggregates, which represent the phase of the basis, are aligned with the five buddhas, which represent the phase of the fruit.

As Sakya Pandita says:

> Initiation is a name given to the technique
> For becoming enlightened in this very lifetime
> After the seeds of buddhahood
> Have been planted within the aggregates,
> Elements and sense-bases.[16]

And:

> Since the Secret Mantra uses dependent origination as
>   its path,
> Its instructions bring the dependent connections into
>   alignment.
> To be ripened by initiation,

> Search for a master whose lineage is unbroken,
> Whose rituals are unconfused,
> Who knows how to arrange the outer and inner
>   dependent originations,
> Who can plant the seeds of the four buddha-bodies
> And who acts in accord with the Buddha's words.
> From him, you should receive the four initiations.[17]

Even in a minor initiation, such as a 'permission initiation', dependent connections are established between the body, speech and mind of a person who receives the initiation and the pure body, speech and mind of the deity of the initiation into which the person is being initiated. Cultivating this connection in meditation, which represents the phase of the path, enables the person to obtain the qualities of the deity's body, speech and mind.

As Sakya Pandita mentioned, for the initiation to have the power to establish this dependent connection, the initiation itself must also embody the process of dependent origination – that is to say, it must come from an unbroken lineage of transmission. If the line of transmission of the initiation has been broken, it no longer has the power to establish these dependent connections and thus the attempt to meditate would be fruitless.

As Sonam Tsemo declares:

> Since the continuum of instruction is unbroken, the meditative concentration of realisation is unbroken.[18]

Dependent origination is also embodied in the interdependence of outer and inner phenomena, which is a vital principle in practising the Vajrayana path. The mind and apparently external phenomena are related through the medium of the subtle body comprising the channels, syllables, drops and winds.

Thus, the outer appearances arise in dependent origination upon the disposition of the elements within the subtle body, and these elements, in turn, arise in dependence upon mind. Likewise, whatever arises in the apparently external world affects the *mandalas* of the subtle body, which, in turn, cause different experiences to arise in mind.

In the process of initiation, for instance, the employment of external objects and activities by the master bring about changes in the inner *mandalas* of the disciple's subtle body. It is for this reason that the initiation must be carried out in accordance with the template provided in the ritual text derived from authentic tantras, because otherwise this relationship of dependent connection is not established. Subsequent to the initiation, practising the methods to which the recipient of the initiation has been introduced will strengthen the connection between outer and inner that has been established in the initiation.

The Vajrayana practitioner, through applying these methods focusing on the interdependence of the outer and inner worlds, will transform his or her experience of the external world.

The following short story from the Sakya tradition illustrates this point. At one time, a yogin was meditating on the completion stage. At the conclusion of his session, he was very thirsty, so he went to the river to drink. However, he could not locate the river where he had imagined it would be. He walked for some time, and, as it became very hot, he put his shawl around the branch of a tree, came back to his dwelling place and fell asleep. On awakening the next morning, he found, to his surprise, that the water was there, exactly where he had previously imagined it to be. In addition, his shawl was hanging on the tree but on the other side of the river. Consequently, he had to get a small boat to cross it to get his shawl back.

On considering this, the yogin realised that the completion stage yogas, upon which he had been meditating the previous day, had temporarily changed the balance of the elements in his body, causing the water element to be suppressed. As a result of this, temporarily the appearance of water had not arisen to him in the seemingly external world. However, once the elements had returned to their habitual state, the appearance of water was evident again.[19]

Such experiences as the one experienced by the meditator in this story are typically only experienced by meditators who have practised diligently for a long time over very many years based on detailed instructions from their Vajrayana masters. However, even those starting out on the Vajrayana path may begin to experience brief glimpses of transformation of perception brought about by meditative practices.

Chapter 7
Patterns in Emptiness

As we begin to experience the dependent nature of the world, through taking the teaching of dependent origination to heart, a sense of lightness and ease develops. We begin to develop a sense of acknowledgement that our existence in the present is part of a continuity, which is both karmic and, as mediated through one's parents, human and cultural.

Yet, at the same time, emptiness, the reality in which birth and death are dissolved, is naturally present at all times in this flow of dependent origination that we call 'life'. So, freedom from whatever burdens we might carry from the past alongside its treasures is always available, but, at the same time, there is no need for resentment, since we need not be imprisoned by it.

Although, from one perspective, the totality of dependent origination seems to suggest that we are all enmeshed in the chains of karma, cause and effect, the very fact that each of these links (or dependent origina-tions) are empty of any solidity means that at any mo-ment we can become free simply by realising this empti-ness.

So we have a 'history': The past is with us – our errors and negative actions on the one hand, and our experi-ence and insights on the other. Yet they are both merely patterns in emptiness and there is no need to feel resent-ment at the past, because, as the chain of causation is empty, it cannot imprison us.

Tragically, we have been our own gaolers, thanks to the fictitious solidity that we attribute both to ourselves and everything we encounter. It is a solidity that is not real since it is founded on the idea that things exist in themselves, isolated and separate in their own boxes. It is the same delusion that causes us to believe that we each exist in a stand-alone bubble. Yet the fragility of this ungrounded sense of self leads us either to attempt to shore it up by absorbing ourselves into some collect-ive entity, whether the state, a class or a movement, or by inventing ever more fanciful identities for our-selves to mask our inner emptiness. Indeed, we become so unmoored from reality that we have unleashed the demons of hatred and factionalism to threaten the dharma itself,[20] as we seek to bend it to our ideological manias.

It is the constant struggle to maintain this delusion of solidity that is the root of all our poisonous emo-tions and suffering. We have pitted ourselves against reality and we can only lose this battle again and again. Thus, by letting go of our cherished delusions, we move beyond the prison wall of our selfishness into a wider life, in which the world is experienced as really is. In the dependent origination of all things, we discover the subtle alignment between outer and inner phenomena – an alignment we might call 'auspicious interdependence' which is, incidentally, the mechanism by which all ritual activity and divinatory techniques work.

Recognising one's contingent nature evokes a tremendous sense of gratitude towards all those upon whose kindness one has depended. Since that kindness itself has no beginning, there can be no end to one's gratitude. The acknowledgement of this immense kindness is the source from which the vast affections of love and compassion spring. In time, it will be these affections that will provide the driving force for achieving buddhahood for others.

Thus a sense of dependent origination prompts the development of wisdom and compassion. This is entirely as it should be, since the dependent origination of all phenomena is the one reality that unites the two truths – ultimate and conventional. The ultimate truth – emptiness beyond all elaborations – is not some higher absolute, beyond conventional truth. Since emptiness and dependent origination are merely two names with one essence, ultimate reality itself is present in the shimmering world of appearances, where emptiness pervades every grain of sand.

As it says in *The Heart of the Perfection of Wisdom Sutra*:

> Form is emptiness, emptiness is form; form is no other than emptiness, emptiness is no other than form.[21]

And as Mipham Rinpoche says:

> Whatever appears is pervaded by emptiness and whatever is empty is pervaded by appearances.[22]

Just as recognising dependent origination reveals the natural unity of the two truths, so it allows us to uncover the perfect balance that exists naturally between continuity and change. It is in this sense that time past is truly included in time present, and time future is contained in both. This is the profound reality that underlies the transmission of the lineages of dharma – a transmission which is nothing other than dependent origination in action.

In fact, when one examines the histories of the great traditions of dharma, one sees a balance of continuity and innovation that reflects the process of dependent origination. Thus the teachings are not modified as they are transmitted from master to disciple, but, nevertheless, there is always a possibility of the teachings being presented in a fresh manner that is appropriate to new situations as they arise. Hence, for instance, Sakya Pandita was the holder of the Sakya lineage of Vajrayana tantras from his guru Jetsun Dragpa Gyaltsen. Yet, unlike his guru, he practised and taught the dharma in a monastic setting. Similarly, one can notice the same blend of continuity and innovation in the early Kagyu lineage as it passes from Milarepa to Gampopa. It is why the Buddha's blessings in the form of his teachings have reached us today with their force undiminished and why the dharma can flourish in the West.

May the lives of my masters, immaculate holders of the Sakya and Kagyu transmissions, remain stable and may their teachings pacify the sufferings of all beings.

OM YE DHARMA HETU PRABHAVA HETUM TESHAM TATHAG-
ATO HYAVADAT TESHAM CHAYO NIRODHA EVAM VADI MAHA
SHRAMANAH SVAHA[23]

May all be auspicious!

Lama Jampa Thaye
London
Miracles Day
3rd March 2018

Appendix

A Note on the Structure of the Dharma

The Systems of Spiritual Practice

The dharma ('Teachings') given by the Buddha in the fifth century BCE encompassed three major 'vehicles' or systems of practice:

1. the Shravakayana ('Vehicle of the Disciples') sometimes known as Hinayana ('The Lesser Vehicle'), which is distinguished by its focus on individual liberation from suffering;

2. the Mahayana ('The Great Vehicle') so called because of its focus on achieving buddhahood for the benefit of all beings; and

3. the Vajrayana ('The Indestructible Vehicle'), which, though it may be regarded as the uncommon Mahayana, is nevertheless a distinct spiritual vehicle in respect of its modes of practice.

The Collections of Scripture

All these teachings given by the Buddha were preserved in literary form in 'The Three Baskets', collected after his passing. This corpus comprises the collection of sutra ('discourses'), primarily concerned with training in meditation, abhidharma ('further dharma'), primarily concerned with training in wisdom, and vinaya ('discipline'), primarily concerned with training in ethics.

The first of these collections, that of the sutra, may be divided into three sections, reflecting the distinct teachings given by Buddha during the periods known as 'The Three Turnings of the Wheel of Dharma' – the first 'Turning of the Wheel' being the presentation of the Shravakayana and the second and third being the presentation of the Mahayana.

The Vajrayana teachings were presented by Buddha Vajradhara and preserved in the scriptures known as the 'tantras'. According to most masters, Indian and Tibetan, the tantras themselves may be grouped in four sets: the kriya, charya, yoga and anuttarayoga classes of tantras. In terms of locating these tantric scriptures, it is most appropriate to regard the tantras as representing a fourth 'basket' of the Buddha's teaching.

The Systems of Tenets

In the centuries following the passing of the Buddha, four major 'systems of tenets' (Skt. *siddhanta*) appeared among his followers in India. These arose out of the need to systematise the philosophical views presented within the collection of scriptures and systems of practice. The first two of these tenet systems, Vaibhashika

('Distinctionists') and Sautrantika ('Sutra Followers'), propounded the teachings characteristic of the Shravakayana, while the Chittamatra ('Mind-Only') and Madhyamaka ('Middle Way') systems elaborated the viewpoint of the Mahayana. Subsequently, all Tibetan masters accepted this four-fold classification of tenets, whilst regarding the Madhyamaka as the supreme system.

Notes

1 'jam mgon Mi pham, *Gateway to Knowledge*, vol. 1 (Rangjung Yeshe: Bodhnath, 1997), 51.

2 Nagarjuna, *Shes pa'i spring yig*, in Karma Thinley Rinpoche, *The Telescope of Wisdom* (Ganesha Press: Bristol, 2009), 118.

3 bSod nams Seng ge, *lTa ba'i shan 'byed theg mchog gnad gyi zla zer* (Sakya Students' Union: Varanasi, n.d.), 67.

4 ibid.

5 'jam mgon Mi pham, op.cit., 57.

6 id., 58.

7 Nagarjuna, op. cit., 112.

8 As quoted in 'jam mgon Ngag dbang Legs pa, 'khor 'das dbyer med gyi lta ba'i snying po bsdus pa skal bzang gi bdud rtsi (hand-written manuscript, n.d.), 3.

9 Maitreya, *Middle Beyond Extremes* (Snow Lion: Ithaca, 2006), 30.

10 Karma pa Rang byung rDo rje, *rNam shes ye shes 'byed pa'i bstan bcos* in Karma Thinley Rinpoche, *The Lamp that Dispels Darkness* (Ganesha Press: Bristol, 2013), 142.

11 Chandrakirti, *Madhyamakavatara* (Khenpo Appey: Gangtok, 1979), 15.

12 id., 20.

13 id., 21.

14 bSod nams rTse mo, *rGyud sde spyi'i rnam par gzhag pa*, in Sa skya'i bka' 'bum, vol. 3 (Ngawang Topgay: New Delhi, 1992), 115.

15 dKon mchog Lhun grub, *rGyud gsum mdzes par 'byed pa'i rgyan* (Phende Rinpoche: New Delhi, n.d.), 9.

16 Sa skya Pandita, *sDom gsum rab tu bye ba'i bstan bcos*, in Sa skya'i bka' 'bum, vol. 12 (Ngawang Topgay: New Delhi, 1992), 35.

17 id., 43.

18 bSod nams rTse mo, op. cit., 117.

19 As related in various *Lam 'bras* sources such as Ngag dbang Legs pa, op. cit, 4.

20 See Lama Jampa Thaye, *Wisdom in Exile: Buddhism and Modern Times* (Ganesha Press: Bristol, 2017), Chapter 4: Politics.

21 *Shes rab snying po'i mdo* in Wa na dpal sa skya'i zhal don phyogs bsdus (Central Institute of Tibetan Higher Studies: Varanasi, 2001), 164-168.

22 'jam mgon Mi pham, *Nges shes rin po che'i sgron me* (Tashi Jong: Palampur, n.d.), 17A.

23 This is the mantra of dependent origination. It was originally presented as the epitome of Buddha's teaching by his disciple Assaji, when asked by Shariputra to summarise the teaching of his master. In translation it means: 'Concerning all phenomena that arise from a cause, the Tathagata (Buddha) has taught their cause and also their cessation.' The mantra can be used to stabilise the blessings generated in one's meditation practice, and, more generally, it is employed to invoke auspiciousness, since the coming-together of all causes and conditions in dependent origination ensures that everything is entirely appropriate.